AF670962

Biblical Abundance

Biblical Abundance

A Scriptural Journey to Financial Freedom

by

David Kamali

FSC
www.fsc.org
MIX
Papper från ansvarsfulla källor
Paper from responsible sources
FSC® C105338

First edition, 2025

Cover photo courtesy of John-Mark Smith via Pexels.

Publisher: BoD · Books on Demand, Östermalmstorg 1, 114 42 Stockholm, bod@bod.se

Print: Libri Plureos GmbH, Friedensallee 273, 22763 Hamburg, Tyskland

ISBN: 978-91-8080-817-0

www.kamaliliterature.com

Contents

Introduction

The thief comes only in order to steal and kill and destroy. I came that they may have and enjoy life, and have it in ***abundance*** *[to the full, till it overflows].*
— John 10:10 (AMP)

I grew up as a Muslim in Iran in a middle-class family. My family was strict, and freedom was limited. To add to the difficulty, my father left us when I was just a child, leaving my mother to raise my brother and me alone. She worked tirelessly as a teacher, but life was tough. There were times when food was scarce, and survival was a daily challenge.

Everything changed when I turned 15. I remember my first year of high school, particularly a Wednesday afternoon during religion class. My teacher made a striking comment about the Quran being the only righteous book, labeling the Bible as corrupt and filled with contradictions. Being a curious and strong-willed teenager in Iran, I was determined to find out why. I headed straight to the library after school, asking for a Bible. The librarian, however, laughed and said, "You know it's illegal to possess a Bible, don't you?"

That moment left me bewildered. If the Bible was truly corrupt, why was it banned? This only deepened my curiosity. Fortunately, I knew a man who sold illegal books, including those about political prisoners during the revolution (I used to buy illegal books related to the revolution from him). I approached him one Friday night and asked if he had a Bible. His initial reaction was suspicion, but when he saw my eagerness, he agreed to help. He led me to a basement shop, where he retrieved a small stack of Bibles from the back. I bought one for about 20,000 IRR, roughly one or two dollars at the time.

As I left, he warned me, "If you're caught with this, you could be arrested or flogged." But I was undeterred. I was determined to read it.

On the bus ride home, I couldn't stop wondering: why was this book so dangerous? That night, I started reading. Months later, as I delved into the Gospel of John, I became convinced that there was only one man worth following: Jesus. That night, I knelt, asking Jesus to be my Lord and Savior. That moment marked a turning point. Life became a "before Jesus" and "after Jesus" journey for me.

At 17, I moved to Sweden to reconnect with my father, who lived there. While I sought acceptance, I fell into the wrong crowd, ignoring the Bible's warnings about corrupt company. By age 20, after countless mistakes that wasted my time, energy, and money, I decided to realign my life with Jesus. I promised to read at least one chapter of the Bible daily and began setting clear goals.

I discovered my talents and pursued them with focus, and by 25, I earned a bachelor's degree in Mathematics, another in English, and a master's degree in Education. Yet, even while walking with God, I lived paycheck to paycheck. I often found myself questioning how biblical figures like David, Job, Solomon, Boaz, and Abraham lived lives of prosperity while I struggled financially. One night, in tears, I cried out to God, asking why I wasn't experiencing the same freedom.

God answered me through His Word: *"Seek first His kingdom and His righteousness, and all these things will be given to you as well"* (Matthew 6:33). I realized that *"seeking"* meant actively pursuing answers in His Word. So, I began an intentional study of the Bible's principles on wealth.

Three years later, at the age of 28, I achieved financial freedom. Now, I'm sharing my journey with you. This book will explore what the Bible teaches about wealth, prosperity, and financial independence. In the final chapter, you'll find a step-by-step guide to financial freedom—the same steps I used to break free from financial stress.

What is Financial Freedom?

Financial freedom means having the resources to cover your living expenses without constantly worrying about your next paycheck. It's about living on your terms and pursuing your God-given purpose without being burdened by financial stress. Here's a simple breakdown:

- **Income > Expenses:** You earn enough to cover your needs and wants without falling into debt.

- **Savings and Investments:** You've built a financial safety net that grows over time, reducing your reliance on work-based income.

- **Choices:** You have the flexibility to spend your time and money as you see fit, whether working, traveling, or serving God.

Financial freedom isn't about being wealthy for wealth's sake—it's about security, peace of mind, and the ability to focus on what truly matters. It empowers you to serve the Lord, support your family, and contribute to meaningful causes.

Why This Book?

The Bible is the ultimate guide to life, including finances. It offers timeless wisdom on how to live a prosperous, honorable, and fulfilling life. Many people chase quick wealth through schemes, courses, or risky investments, but they ignore the principles laid out in Scripture.

Throughout this book, I'll show you how biblical figures applied God's principles to achieve generational wealth. Even today, we see the lasting financial influence of the Jewish community, which faithfully follows the teachings of the Old Testament.

Each chapter of this book will guide you through practical applications of God's Word for your finances. At the end of every chapter, you'll find simple reflection questions. Take time to write down your answers, and by the end of the book, you'll see a transformation in how you approach your finances.

My Prayer for You

I pray that these chapters speaks to you as you read. I pray that God answers your financial questions and blesses you abundantly, according to His purpose for your life. May you experience His provision and use your blessings to uplift others. When people look at your life, may they say, "Surely, this is someone God has blessed."

Let's begin this journey to financial freedom, rooted in God's eternal truth.

1 Created in God's Image

"So God created mankind in his own image, in the image of God he created them; male and female he created them."
— Genesis 1:27

With no reference point, God spoke the heavens and the earth into existence. His Word shaped the stars, the seas, the trees, and the clouds—everything that exists was born from His command. Yet, in all His majesty and power, He chose to create mankind in His own image, the ultimate reflection of His essence.

We are the only creation formed with God's own likeness, the only time He used Himself as a model. And He didn't stop there—He breathed His Spirit into us, imparting a piece of Himself into His most precious creation.

But why is this significant?
When God created everything else, He didn't breathe life into them; His Word was enough. Yet, with us, He went beyond. This wasn't an accident or coincidence—it's a divine revelation. God was showing us something profound: *We were created to reflect Him, to carry His nature, and to walk in His power.*

Bearing the Image of God

Imagine this: a fruit bears the seed of the tree that produced it. Just as the fruit reflects the tree, we reflect the Creator. This means every characteristic of God is mirrored in us:

- God loves; we are called to love.
- God feels; we experience emotions.
- God works; we are made to work.
- God rests; we, too, need rest.
- God creates; we are designed to create.

This divine resemblance is not just a metaphor; it's a call to action.

Your Inheritance as God's Child

As believers, we are not merely God's creation—we are His children. Throughout the Bible, we see that a father's wealth becomes the inheritance of his children. God, who owns everything, has made us heirs to His blessings, wisdom, and abundance.

The promise is clear: *"For those who are led by the Spirit of God are the children of God"* (Romans 8:14). We are entitled to walk in His favor, His provision, and His peace.

Understanding this changes everything. You no longer see yourself as limited by your circumstances; you recognize that your potential is rooted in the infinite power of your Creator.

Applying God's Character in Your Life

In the chapters ahead, we'll dive deeper into the attributes of God and explore how His nature can be reflected in your daily life. By aligning yourself with God's principles and character, you'll unlock the keys to prosperity and financial freedom.

Remember, every step you take in faith prepares you for the final chapters of this book, where we'll translate God's principles into actionable steps. These steps will not only lead to financial independence but also a life of purpose and fulfillment.

To Do:

- See yourself as a beloved child of God.
- Believe in your God-given potential.
- Trust God's timing and His plans for your life.
- Start each day affirming that you are created to do great things.

Reflection Question:

If you are created in God's image, with His Spirit dwelling within you, and your spiritual DNA reflecting His nature, don't you think your Heavenly Father wants you to live a life of peace, purpose, and abundance—just as He does?

2 God the Giver of Wisdom, Wealth, and Honor

"Moreover, I will give you what you have not asked for—both wealth and honor—so that in your lifetime you will have no equal among kings."
— 1 Kings 3:13

When God spoke to Solomon, He offered him the chance to ask for anything. Solomon could have requested power, riches, or even dominion over the kingdoms of the world, and God would have granted it. But Solomon understood something profound: material wealth alone does not bring lasting fulfillment or generational impact. Instead, he asked for wisdom to lead God's people.

God was so pleased with Solomon's request that He not only granted him unmatched wisdom but also blessed him with wealth and honor beyond compare.

This passage contains deep, transformative lessons, but let's focus on the source of Solomon's wealth and prosperity. The key takeaway is this: *God is not only the source of wisdom; He is also the source of wealth, honor, and enduring prosperity.*

As Proverbs 8:18 reminds us, *"With me are riches and honor, enduring wealth and prosperity."* When you seek God's wisdom, you position yourself to receive favor, honor, and the blessings of abundance. By remaining close to Him—the ultimate source of all good things—you allow His guidance to shape every decision, leading to a life marked by fruitfulness and success.

Wisdom: The Foundation of Abundance

Through wisdom, God provides us with insight, clarity, and discernment for life's challenges. Wisdom is the foundation upon which enduring wealth and honor are built. Proverbs 9:11 tells us, *"For through wisdom your days will be many, and years will be added to your life."*

Remember, seeking wisdom is not just about gaining knowledge but applying godly principles in your daily life. As you grow in wisdom, your life aligns more closely with God's plan, and His blessings naturally follow.

My Journey Back to Wisdom

There was a time when I lived recklessly, making poor decisions and ignoring God's guidance. It wasn't until I, like the prodigal son, returned to Him that my life began to change. One night, I cried out to God, asking Him to take control of my life once more. In His infinite mercy, He embraced me with open arms.

That encounter with God was life-changing. His Spirit gave me the wisdom to recognize what I needed to leave behind—the habits, relationships, and choices that were holding me back. While the decision to walk away from those things was mine, it was God's wisdom and strength that empowered me to take that step.

Looking back, I'm deeply grateful that I chose to surrender to Him. Without that pivotal decision, I wouldn't be where I am today.

To Do:

- Begin each morning by thanking God and asking Him to increase your wisdom.
- Pray for His guidance in your decisions and for favor and honor in your interactions.
- Trust that God's wisdom will lead you toward a life of prosperity and purpose.

Reflection Question:

If you were in Solomon's position, standing before the Lord with the chance to ask for anything, what would you request?

If your answer focuses on material possessions, pause for a moment. While God can certainly bless you with wealth, consider the greater treasures He offers—wisdom, favor, and honor. These are the keys to a life of lasting impact and generational blessings.

3 God the Planner

"For I know the plans I have for you," declares the Lord, "plans to prosper you and not to harm you, plans to give you hope and a future."
— Jeremiah 29:11

Just as we carefully plan our daily lives, God has divine plans for each of us. We're not here by chance or coincidence; every life has a purpose, and God's plans are filled with hope, prosperity, and meaning.

Before you were born, God envisioned a life for you that reflects His goodness and glory. He desires for you to live a life of purpose, overflowing with His blessings. The Bible reminds us that God has already opened the doors of heaven for His children, saying, *"Ask, and it will be given to you"* (Matthew 7:7). Trust Him and His perfect plans for your life.

God Is a Master Planner

God doesn't act randomly. From the creation of the universe to the smallest details of our lives, everything unfolds according to His divine plan. In the same way, He calls us to be planners too. Planning is a mark of faith and stewardship, but our plans must align with His will.

How can we ensure our plans reflect God's purpose? The answer lies in His Word. If your plans are rooted in Scripture and align with godly principles, they are more likely to bear fruit. For example, a plan to enrich yourself through dishonesty or harm others is destined to fail. But if your plan involves pursuing education, serving your community, or building a business that glorifies God and benefits others, you're on the right path.

A Personal Testimony of God's Faithfulness

There was a time when I tried to follow my own plans, only to face failure and frustration. But one night, I decided to surrender my ambitions to God. With a pen and paper in hand, I prayed for guidance and began writing down my goals.

I listed everything I wanted: pursuing higher education, earning my degrees, traveling, and building meaningful connections. I trusted God's promise and started applying to universities. In His faithfulness, He opened the exact doors I prayed for, leading me to the programs and institutions I'd hoped for.

This experience reinforced an essential truth: when we commit our plans to God, He directs our steps and ensures success according to His perfect will.

The Power of Writing Your Plans

Writing down your plans is not just an act of organization—it's an act of faith. It shows God that you trust Him with your desires and are willing to work toward them. Habakkuk 2:2 (NKJV) says, *"Write the vision and make it plain on tablets, that he may run who reads it."* By putting your plans on paper, you clarify your vision, stay focused, and allow God to work through your faith and obedience.

To Do:

- Pray for wisdom and guidance.
- Write down your goals and the steps needed to achieve them.
- Include your desires and ask God to fulfill them according to His will.
- Believe in His promises and trust Him to provide the resources and opportunities.

Reflection Question:

Do you have a dream or goal that keeps you awake at night? Perhaps it's completing your education, starting a business, or pursuing a passion that God has placed in your heart. What's holding you back from taking the first step?

4 God the Hard Worker

"In the beginning God created the heavens and the earth."

— Genesis 1:1

The opening line of any book sets the tone for everything that follows, and the Bible is no exception. It begins with action—God creating the heavens and the earth. The Bible doesn't open by saying that God sat on His throne and rested; instead, it shows Him at work, crafting and shaping the universe. From the very first verse, we see that God is a diligent worker with a clear vision, purpose, and the determination to bring it to life.

Creating something is no small feat; it requires focus, energy, and dedication. The first thing God reveals about Himself in Scripture is His work ethic. If God—our Creator—began with hard work, how much more should we, His children, follow His example?

Laziness Is Contrary to God's Design

God detests laziness because it contradicts His nature and purpose for us. In the parable of the talents, Jesus describes a servant who, out of fear and laziness, buried his talent instead of working to multiply it. The master called this servant *"wicked and lazy"* (Matthew 25:26). Laziness, in God's eyes, is not merely an inconvenience—it is wickedness because it squanders the gifts, talents, and opportunities He has given us.

We are created to work diligently and serve God's purpose through our efforts. Hard work is not about hustling for personal gain alone but about fulfilling God's plan and serving others in the process.

Planning Leads to Action

In the last chapter, we discussed the importance of planning. Now it's time to take those plans and put them into action. Notice that God didn't rest on the first day and begin creating on the second—He started His work immediately. Likewise, don't delay; start working on your goals today. In fact, start now!

A Personal Testimony of Hard Work

Hard work has been a cornerstone of my life. During my university years, I worked part-time as a teaching assistant while managing my studies. As soon as I graduated, I secured a full-time position as a mathematics teacher. These experiences taught me the value of diligence and perseverance. Hard work not only opens doors but also refines character and builds resilience.

To Do:

- If you're currently working: Pray over your job. Ask God for favor, wisdom, and opportunities to be a positive influence in your workplace. Look for ways to grow and serve others through your work. Consider learning a new skill or starting a side hustle to increase your income and broaden your experience.
- If you're a student: Pray for your studies, and start building discipline by taking on a small part-time job or gig. This will not only help you grow financially but also teach you valuable life skills.
- If you're unemployed: Pray that God will bring the right people and opportunities into your life. Apply for at least 50 jobs a day and persist until you secure a position, no matter how small. While you're job hunting, invest in yourself by learning new skills that can open more doors.
- If you're a business owner: Pray for your business and seek God's guidance on how to expand. Explore new markets, cities, or even countries. Let your business be a reflection of God's glory as you thrive and shine.

Reflection Question:

When God created human beings, He gave them meaningful work—cultivating the garden and naming the animals. Don't you think He created you with a unique purpose and work to fulfill as well?

5 God the Master of Skills

"And I have filled him with the Spirit of God, with wisdom, with understanding, with knowledge and with all kinds of skills—to make artistic designs for work in gold, silver and bronze, to cut and set stones, to work in wood, and to engage in all kinds of crafts."
— Exodus 31:3-5

When we are filled with the Holy Spirit, we receive more than just wisdom and understanding; we are also blessed with unique skills and talents. These are gifts from God, given to us not only for personal fulfillment but also to serve His purpose and bless others.

Every skill and talent is like a seed. It can either be nurtured and developed, bearing fruit, or neglected and wasted. To achieve financial freedom and a life of purpose, it's vital to recognize and cultivate the gifts God has given us.

Using Your Skills for God's Glory

God has equipped each of us with specific skills. You might have a gift for music, art, cooking, teaching, organizing, or even photography. These skills are not random; they are divine tools meant to bless others and glorify God.

When we use our talents in service to God and His people, we open ourselves to His blessings in return.

Take my own journey as an example. I've always enjoyed photography and videography, but for years, I didn't see it as a gift or a potential avenue for success. That changed when someone recognized my talent and encouraged me to pursue it. Once I began developing my skills, I turned them into a business that not only blessed others but also helped me achieve financial freedom.

I've also seen people who were gifted in singing start in their church choirs, gradually growing in confidence and skill. Today, they travel from city to city, singing gospel songs and spreading God's message.

The God we serve is a fair and generous God. If He has given me a gift, He has given you one too—perhaps even more than one. But it's up to you to discover, develop, and use your gift for His glory.

Developing Your Skills

Recognizing your gift is just the first step. To truly honor God with your talents, you must put in the effort to grow and refine them. Educate yourself. Seek opportunities to practice and learn more. Whether through formal education, online courses, mentorship, or hands-on experience, invest in your skills.

Once you've developed your gift, consider turning it into a side hustle. This allows you to earn income while using your skills to serve others. A side hustle not only accelerates your journey to financial freedom but also demonstrates faithful stewardship of what God has entrusted to you.

To Do:

- Take time to reflect on your abilities. What are you naturally good at, and how can this gift be used to bless others?
- Once you identify your gift, commit to developing it. Research, practice, and seek guidance to sharpen your skills.
- Begin using your skill in practical ways. Start a side hustle or volunteer your talent in your community or church. Watch how God blesses your efforts as you faithfully use your gifts.

Reflection Question:

Do you remember the parable of the king and his three servants in the Bible? (Matthew 25:14-30) Each servant was given talents, and their actions determined how the king responded upon his return. Now reflect: you are one of those servants. What will you do with the talents and gifts God has entrusted to you?

6 God the Creator

"Isn't this the carpenter's son? Isn't his mother's name Mary, and aren't his brothers James, Joseph, Simon and Judas?"
— Matthew 13:55

God, in all His majesty and ownership of the universe, chose to dwell among us in the form of His Son, Jesus Christ. What did Jesus do while on earth? He worked. Not only did He serve as a spiritual leader, but He also took on a profession as a carpenter, following in Joseph's footsteps. Jesus was skillful, diligent, and resourceful in His craft, demonstrating both the value of hard work and the importance of practical skills.

Also, Jesus was serving a greater purpose. When the Roman soldiers crucified Him, they used nails and a hammer to fasten Him to a wooden cross. Nails, wood, hammers—these are the very tools a carpenter uses to build. They may have thought they were tearing Him down, but little did they know, they were building Him up.

From Skills to Business

The example Jesus set is one we should follow. Once you've developed your skills—whether in carpentry, painting, music, or another area—you can begin using them to create value. But don't stop there. Take the next step and establish a business based on those skills.

Owning a business allows you to reflect God's character as a creator. Isaiah 40:28 reminds us, *"Do you not know? Have you not heard? The Lord is the everlasting God, the Creator of the ends of the earth."* When you create a business, you're not only building something tangible but also fulfilling God's creative nature in your own life.

Practical Steps to Launch Your Business

Starting a business might seem intimidating, but it's a vital step toward financial freedom and leaving a lasting legacy for your children. Here are the steps:

1. Register Your Business: Identify the type of business that suits you, whether it's a sole proprietorship, a partnership, or a corporation. Register it with the proper authorities in your country.
2. Name Your Business: Choose a name that reflects your mission and vision.
3. Set Up the Essentials: Create a bank account for your business and build an online presence with a simple website or social media profile.
4. Start Small: Even if it's a freelance or side business, the key is to start. Remember, great things often have humble beginnings.

This step is critical for achieving financial freedom. A business not only multiplies your earnings but also positions you to bless others—individuals and businesses alike.

Overcoming Fear and Skepticism

Many people are hesitant to start a business. Some doubt its importance, while others believe only entrepreneurs succeed financially. Both mindsets are flawed. The Bible offers wisdom in Ecclesiastes 11:6:

Sow your seed in the morning, and at evening let your hands not be idle, for you do not know which will succeed, whether this or that, or whether both will do equally well.

This verse highlights the importance of balance. Your 9-to-5 job (sowing in the morning) and your business (working in the evening) are both valuable. Each plays a unique role in your journey toward financial independence.

My Personal Experience

I followed this principle in my own life. While working full-time as a teacher, I also taught privately and pursued my passion for photography. Eventually, I turned my photography into a business. That business grew beyond my expectations, reaching international clients and creating opportunities I never imagined.

God blesses hard work and wise stewardship. Taking the step to launch a business may feel daunting, but it's a step worth taking.

To Do:

- Pray for clarity, guidance, and the courage to start your business.
- Research the type of business that best suits your skills and goals.
- Register your business, name it, and set up a professional presence (bank account, website, etc.).
- Begin building your network. Introduce yourself and offer your services for free initially, as an act of service and faith. Trust that God will multiply your clients and your impact.

Reflection Question:

You've likely seen internet gurus claiming that working a 9-to-5 is a trap, encouraging you to join their course to "get rich quick." What do you think of their advice? Here's my perspective: such teachings often miss the deeper principles of life and Scripture. Biblically speaking, work is foundational to humanity. It's the first thing God did! Building wealth requires saving, investing, and creating value, which often starts with working a job to accumulate the capital necessary to launch a business. God's principles are simple and effective: work hard, steward well, and trust Him with the increase.

7 God the Provider

"So Abraham called that place The Lord Will Provide. And to this day it is said, 'On the mountain of the Lord it will be provided.'"
— Genesis 22:14

Abraham understood a profound truth about God: He is Jehovah-Jireh, the Lord who provides. God, in His very nature, is a provider, just as a loving father provides for his household. This characteristic of God is foundational to understanding how we, too, can rely on Him to meet our needs. When you embark on your journey toward financial freedom, remember that it is through the Lord's favor that your work and business flourish.

When I started my own business, I was filled with fear and uncertainty. The first few months were challenging, with barely any clients. But I held on to my faith and continually prayed for God's provision. I also committed to using my business to bless others without expecting immediate payment. Within a month, I landed my first deals, and within a year, I was traveling across Europe with some of the biggest artists in the world as their photographer and videographer.

One scripture that gave me strength during those times was *"Noah found favor in the eyes of the Lord"* (Genesis 6:8). I believe that no one can truly succeed in life without finding favor with God. Thankfully, He is a generous God who delights in blessing those who walk faithfully with Him.

Freedom from Debt

As a provider, God desires for you to live in freedom, including financial freedom. The Bible says in Proverbs 22:7, *"The rich rule over the poor, and the borrower is slave to the lender."* God doesn't want you to be burdened by debt. Instead, He wants you to experience the liberty that comes with being debt-free. Biblically, one of the steps toward financial independence is to *"give to everyone what you owe them"* (Romans 13:7). Paying off debt is not only practical but also aligns with God's principles. To help you achieve this, I'll share the exact method I used to pay off my debts and become financially free.

The Debt Repayment Plan

Step 1: List Your Debts

Write down all your debts, starting with the smallest amount and moving to the largest. Be specific about the monthly payments you make for each. For example:

- Debt 1: $3,500 with a monthly payment of $300
- Debt 2: $6,600 with a monthly payment of $300
- Debt 3: $9,000 with a monthly payment of $400

Step 2: Earn Extra Income

Use your side hustle or business to generate at least $200 in additional monthly income. This extra money will accelerate your debt repayment.

Start by applying the extra $200 to your smallest debt. In my case, I added $200 to my $300 monthly payment for Debt 1, paying $500 monthly instead.

New payment structure:

- Debt 1: $3,500 with a monthly payment of *$500*
- Debt 2: $6,900 with a monthly payment of $300
- Debt 3: $9,000 with a monthly payment of $400

Step 3: Pay Off the First Debt

Continue paying down the smallest debt with the extra $200 until it's fully paid. For me, this took ***seven months***. Here's what my debts looked like afterward:

- Debt 1: Paid off
- Debt 2: $4,800 with a monthly payment of $300
- Debt 3: $6,200 with a monthly payment of $400

Step 4: Apply the First Debt Payment to the Second

Once Debt 1 was fully paid off, I added the $500 I had been paying on Debt 1 to the $300 monthly payment for Debt 2. My new payment structure became:

- Debt 1: Paid off
- Debt 2: $4,800 with a monthly payment of *$800*
- Debt 3: $6,200 with a monthly payment of $400

Step 5: Pay Off the Second Debt

I continued paying $800 a month for Debt 2 and cleared it in ***six months***. My updated debt situation was:

- Debt 1: Paid off
- Debt 2: Paid off
- Debt 3: $3,800 with a monthly payment of $400

Step 6: Apply All Payments to the Last Debt

Finally, I combined the $800 from Debt 2 with the $400 monthly payment for Debt 3, paying $1,200 monthly. This allowed me to pay off the last debt in just ***three months***.

In total, it took me **16 months** to become completely debt-free, saving time and interest compared to the typical repayment schedule.

Key Takeaway

No matter how many debts you have, follow this method faithfully, and you'll achieve freedom from financial bondage. Once you're debt-free, commit to staying that way. Avoid taking on new debts and focus on building wealth God's way.

To Do

Take a pen and paper, list all your debts in order from smallest to largest, and implement this method immediately. Be disciplined and dedicated. Paying off your debts in full is not only a practical necessity but also a biblical principle essential for financial freedom.

Reflection Question

Can you name a biblical character who wholeheartedly followed God but owed people money? Think about it—God's followers are called to live in freedom, not bondage. What steps will you take today to ensure you live a debt-free life?

8 God the Investor

"So he called ten of his servants and gave them ten minas. 'Put this money to work,' he said, 'until I come back.'"
— Luke 19:13

One of the most inspiring aspects of God's nature is that He is an investor. He invested His time and power to create the universe, and He continues to invest in us, desiring a deep relationship with His children.

As we seek financial freedom, our next step is to embrace the principle of investing. Jesus Himself emphasized this in the parable of the ten minas (A mina was about three months' wages), where the king instructed his servants to *"put this money to work."* This is a clear call to invest, not merely to save. In fact, the servant who buried his money—essentially saving it without any growth—was rebuked and called *wicked and lazy*.

God Calls Us to Be Investors, Not Mere Savers

Investing allows us to multiply what God has entrusted to us, aligning with His desire for us to grow and prosper. Saving, while important for emergencies, doesn't allow your money to work for you or grow over time. As stewards of God's blessings, we are called to put our resources into fruitful ventures that generate returns.

Where Should You Invest?

You may wonder, *"What should I invest in?"* The answer lies in what God has blessed throughout Scripture. Haggai 2:8 reminds us, *"The silver is mine and the gold is mine,' declares the Lord Almighty."* These precious metals have stood the test of time, retaining their value through centuries.

The Bible also speaks of blessings in land, fields, livestock, and resources like timber and iron. Applying these principles today, consider investing in:

- **Gold and Silver:** These are God's enduring assets. They are God's money.
- **Real Estate:** Land and property remain valuable investments.
- **Commodities:** Livestock, energy, and essential materials reflect biblical principles of prosperity.
- **Index Funds or ETFs:** Focus on sectors aligned with God's provision, such as agriculture, energy, and technology.

My Personal Experience

After paying off my debts, I began implementing this principle. I committed to investing 20% of my income in silver, gold, and index funds focused on real estate, livestock, technology and energy. This diversified portfolio helped me grow my wealth steadily and achieve my financial freedom goals.

Biblical Wisdom on Investing

Remember, investing isn't about chasing trends or get-rich-quick schemes. These often lead to dishonest gains, which the Bible warns against: *"Dishonest money dwindles away, but whoever gathers money little by little makes it grow"* (Proverbs 13:11). Stay faithful to biblical principles, and trust in God's provision and timing.

To Do

- **Build an Emergency Fund:** After paying off your debts, save at least three months' worth of fixed expenses. This ensures you won't need to borrow again in case of unforeseen circumstances.
- **Invest 20% of Your Income:** Start allocating a portion of your monthly income into God's money—gold, silver, and other biblically endorsed assets.
- **Avoid Dishonest or Risky Ventures:** Stay away from companies or trends that exploit others or promise instant riches. Seek investments that align with God's principles and bring lasting value.

Reflection Question

Have you ever studied the long-term value of gold and silver? These assets have stood firm throughout history, just as God's faithfulness never fails His children. What steps will you take today to start investing in "God's money"?

9 From Obedience to Abundance

"Submit to God and be at peace with him; in this way prosperity will come to you."
— Job 22:21

The God we serve is a God of peace, even in the midst of life's storms. You've now reached a major milestone: you're debt-free and have established a portfolio of passive income through your investments. However, challenges will arise, including fluctuations in the market that may tempt you to worry.

Resist the urge to check your investments constantly or panic when the market dips. Instead, submit your life and your financial decisions to God. Trust Him to bless your efforts and grow your wealth over time. Patience and faith are key. Let the power of compounding work its magic. Over decades, your investments will build generational wealth for your family, and God may even surprise you with unexpected blessings sooner than you think.

The Promise of Prosperity

"Walk in obedience to all that the Lord your God has commanded you, so that you may live and prosper and prolong your days in the land that you will possess."
— Deuteronomy 5:33

God's promises are as true today as they were in ancient times. When you walk in obedience to His Word, you align yourself with His principles for a prosperous and fulfilling life. This truth is universal, whether you live in Canada, Sweden, or anywhere else. God's principles transcend borders and cultures.

I've seen this promise fulfilled in my own life, and I can confidently testify that God honors those who walk faithfully with Him. Obedience is the key that unlocks the door to abundance.

A God of Overflowing Blessings

"You will nurse and be satisfied at her comforting breasts; you will drink deeply and delight in her overflowing abundance."
— Isaiah 66:11

God doesn't simply meet the needs of His children; He blesses them abundantly. When He opens the floodgates of heaven, He pours out blessings beyond measure. But these blessings come through obedience, trust, and patience.

As you grow in your walk with Him, trust that He desires for you to enjoy the fruits of your labor. God delights in seeing His children prosper—not just financially but in every area of life. Ask Him daily for guidance, and watch as His hand moves in your favor.

To Do

- **Submit Your Investments to God:** Pray over your portfolio and trust Him to bless and grow it over time.
- **Resist Panic:** Avoid making hasty financial decisions based on fear. Markets fluctuate, but God's provision is constant.
- **Walk in Obedience:** Stay faithful to God's Word and principles in all areas of your life, including your finances.
- **Keep the Long-Term Vision:** Focus on building generational wealth through consistent, wise investments.

Reflection Question

Can you trust God to guide your financial journey, even in times of uncertainty? How does submitting your life and resources to Him bring peace and prosperity?

10 What Is Required of Me and You

"He has shown you, O mortal, what is good. And what does the Lord require of you? To act justly and to love mercy and to walk humbly with your God."
— Micah 6:8

Now that you've achieved financial freedom—becoming debt-free, with investments generating income to cover your fixed costs and lifestyle—it's time to ask: *Now what?* This chapter explores essential characteristics of God that provide guidance for the next phase of your journey.

Essence 1: A Hard-Working God

"All hard work brings a profit, but mere talk leads only to poverty."
— Proverbs 14:23

We've already discussed God as a hard worker, but this principle remains relevant even after achieving financial independence. Financial freedom provides more time for family, friends, and serving others, but it doesn't mean we stop working. We were created for work.

Even after I became financially free, I didn't stop working. In fact, I worked more—but with a renewed purpose. A part of my work became voluntary, and the blessings I received were greater than before.

Don't quit your job or shut down your business. Instead, continue to refine and grow. You may reduce your working hours, but remember, you're building generational wealth. As Lamentations 5:19 reminds us: *"You, Lord, reign forever; your throne endures from generation to generation."* Your business, too, can endure for generations if you remain diligent.

Essence 2: A Generous God

"Honor the Lord with your wealth, with the firstfruits of all your crops; then your barns will be filled to overflowing, and your vats will brim over with new wine."

— Proverbs 3:9-10

Generosity is at the heart of God's character. He gives freely, holding nothing back—not even His only Son. As His children, we are called to reflect this generosity.

Once you've reached financial independence, don't turn away from those in need. Generosity isn't limited to money; it can also involve time, skills, or resources.

For example, if you're skilled in painting and notice your neighbor's house needs a fresh coat of paint, offer your help without expecting payment. I knew a man who worked as a cleaner, and he cleaned his church every Sunday for free. God's favor was upon him, and he was promoted to a leadership position at the company he worked.

Jesus said, *"Give, and it will be given to you. A good measure, pressed down, shaken together and running over, will be poured into your lap"* (Luke 6:38). I've experienced this firsthand. Once, I paid for several young people to attend a church camp. Though it cost me only $100, within days, I received a bonus worth more than 100 times that amount. God rewards those who give cheerfully.

Start by giving 10% of your income to a church that preaches the Bible. Malachi 3:10 is the only place in Scripture where God says, *"Test me in this."*

Essence 3: A Humble God

"Take my yoke upon you and learn from me, for I am gentle and humble in heart, and you will find rest for your souls."
— Matthew 11:29

True rest comes from God, not from wealth or investments. While financial freedom may bring a more comfortable life, it's only in God that we find lasting peace and fulfillment.

Even in my financial independence, I remain fully dependent on God. I never boast about my wealth because I know it's a result of His blessings. Instead, I direct people to the Bible. I encourage everyone, including unbelievers, to read it—even if only as a history book. The Word of God changes lives.

Essence 4: A Fair and Faithful God

"The Almighty is beyond our reach and exalted in power; in his justice and great righteousness, he does not oppress."
— Job 37:23

God is a fair and just God. Everything He does is righteous. Fairness is an essential characteristic for us to practice, especially in business.

As a teacher and business owner, I've made fairness a cornerstone of my work, and it has brought hidden blessings. The Bible says, *"Let us hold unswervingly to the hope we profess, for he who promised is faithful"* (Hebrews 10:23). God always keeps His promises, and His faithfulness is a model for how we should live and work.

One practice I've adopted is personalizing biblical blessings. When I read about God blessing Abraham, I replace his name with mine, trusting that God's promises apply to me as well. Faith is the key that unlocks these blessings.

In your business, practice integrity. If you promise to fix Mr. Joe's car but Mrs. Jane asks for your help at the same time, honor your commitment to Mr. Joe first. This builds trust and a reputation for honesty. As 1 Chronicles 29:17 says, *"I know, my God, that you test the heart and are pleased with integrity."*

To Do

- **Keep working:** Even after reaching financial freedom, stay engaged in meaningful work, whether for income, personal growth, or service to others.
- **Be generous:** Give back to your community, church, and those in need. Start tithing if you haven't already.
- **Stay humble:** Acknowledge that all blessings come from God, and use your position to point others to Him.
- **Practice fairness and faithfulness:** Be a person of integrity in your personal and professional life.

Reflection Question

How can you reflect God's hard work, generosity, humility, and fairness in your daily life, especially now that you've reached financial freedom?

11 Warnings About Wealth

"By your wisdom and understanding you have gained wealth for yourself and amassed gold and silver in your treasuries. By your great skill in trading you have increased your wealth, and because of your wealth your heart has grown proud. Therefore this is what the Sovereign Lord says: 'Because you think you are wise, as wise as a god, I am going to bring foreigners against you, the most ruthless of nations; they will draw their swords against your beauty and wisdom and pierce your shining splendor.'"
— Ezekiel 28:4-7

I would be remiss if I only spoke about the benefits of wealth without addressing the dangers it can bring. My dear friend, whether you are on the path to financial independence or have already reached your goals, remember this: wealth is a powerful tool, but it can also be a dangerous trap if not handled with care.

Wealth as a Servant, Not a Master

Always view your wealth as a servant, never as a master. The only Master we serve is God Almighty. No possession, no amount of money, should ever take His place in your life. Wealth is a resource to be stewarded, not a god to be worshiped.

Thankfully, God has given us the Holy Spirit to guide us and His Word to act as a mirror, reflecting any red flags that may arise in our hearts.

Red Flags to Watch For

1. **A Proud Heart**

   If you reach your financial goals and find yourself thinking that you no longer need God, take heed. This is a warning sign that pride is creeping in. Wealth can deceive us into believing we are self-sufficient, but nothing could be further from the truth.

2. **A Closed Hand**

   If you start to feel reluctant about giving and instead want to hoard or reinvest every dollar, pause. Remember that the principle of sowing and reaping applies here: *"Give, and it will be given to you"* (Luke 6:38).

3. **Reckless Spending**

   If you're tempted to use your wealth on extravagant or ungodly pursuits—wild living, risky schemes, or questionable investments—stop and turn your heart back to God. The enemy often uses wealth as a tool for temptation. Stay vigilant.

Wise Stewardship

There's nothing wrong with enjoying the blessings God has given you. Buying a new car or taking a family vacation can be a wonderful way to enjoy your financial freedom. But remember: these decisions must be made wisely. Never dip into your emergency fund or sell your investments to fund unnecessary luxuries. Let the dividends or profits from your investments cover these expenses.

The key is balance. Use your wealth to glorify God, bless others, and create a stable future for your family. Keep your heart humble and your focus on God, and He will continue to guide you.

To Do

- **Reflect:** Ask the Holy Spirit to reveal any pride, greed, or unhealthy attachments to your wealth.
- **Stay Accountable:** Surround yourself with godly mentors who can provide guidance and correction.
- **Remain Generous:** Continue giving faithfully, knowing that generosity is both a blessing and a safeguard against greed.

Reflection Question

What steps can you take today to ensure that wealth remains a servant in your life, and not a master?

12 Faith and Flourish

Congratulations! You've made it to the final chapter. By now, you've learned the principles of financial freedom rooted in God's Word. It's time to take what you've learned and apply it—not just for your benefit, but to help others flourish as well. Share this journey with your friends and family, and encourage them to follow these steps to achieve financial independence.

Step-by-Step Guide to Financial Freedom

1. **Pray for Wisdom and Guidance and Start Planning**
   Begin by asking God for wisdom and allowing the Holy Spirit to guide you. This journey isn't just about financial freedom; it's about living a life that honors God. Start writing down your plans and everything you want from God.

2. **Get to Work—Today**
   Whether it's a 9-to-5 job as a cleaner, teacher, nurse, or CEO, start working today. Laziness is a dangerous trap, and hard work honors God. If you're a student, take on a part-time job—even just four hours a week. It will teach you discipline and provide extra income. Remember, work for the Lord, not just for the paycheck.

3. **Learn a Skill**
   While working your 9-to-5, dedicate time to learning a skill. It

could be painting, baking, photography, coding, or even car polishing. Choose a skill that aligns with your interests and put in the effort to master it.

4. **Start a Business**

   Use your skill to start a business. Register it, offer your services, and begin earning. Start by serving your community and don't be discouraged by slow growth. Even one sale a month can lead to greater opportunities. Serve others wholeheartedly, and God will bless your efforts. Aim to make at least $200 extra each month from your side hustle.

5. **Pay Off All Debts**

   Use the debt repayment method outlined in this book to clear your debts quickly. Becoming debt-free is crucial to financial freedom.

6. **Start Investing**

   Once you're debt-free, begin investing 20% of your income. Forget the 50/30/20 rule and follow this instead: 50/20/20/10 Rule

   - **50%: Fixed expenses** (rent, utilities, food).
   - **20%: Personal wants** (dining out, travel, clothing).
   - **20%: Investments.** Focus on God's money—gold, silver, real estate, and low-fee index funds.
   - **10%: Tithe.** This is your partnership with God, who blesses those who give with a cheerful heart (Malachi 3:10).

7. **Additional Tips:**

   Build an emergency fund covering three to six months of fixed expenses before investing heavily. Never touch your emergency fund unless it's a true emergency. Replenish it immediately if used.

8. **Reduce Fixed Expenses Over Time**

   As your investments grow, aim to reduce your fixed expenses from 50% to 40% of your income. This will allow your portfolio to grow faster and provide greater financial flexibility.

Final Thoughts

Remember, financial freedom is not the end goal—it's a means to serve God and others more effectively. By walking in faith, taking consistent steps, and trusting God's provision, you will flourish in every area of your life.

Reflection Question

What steps will you take today to begin or continue your journey to financial freedom, and how can you use your resources to honor God and bless others?

Afterword

"The earth is the Lord's, and everything in it, the world, and all who live in it."
— Psalm 24:1

As we close this journey, I want to remind you of one vital truth: everything you have, and everything you will ever achieve, comes from God. He is the source of your strength, your wisdom, and your provision. Every principle in this book, every lesson learned, points back to Him.

You've walked through 12 chapters of practical, biblical steps to achieve financial freedom. From working diligently, discovering your God-given skills, and starting a business, to paying off debt, investing wisely, and walking in generosity—each step has brought you closer to living a life of purpose, peace, and abundance.

But financial freedom is not just about wealth. It's about stewardship, obedience, and trust in God's plan. It's about becoming a vessel through which God's blessings flow, not just into your life but into the lives of others.

Stay Humble, Stay Faithful

As you enjoy the fruits of your labor and God's blessings, stay humble. Wealth has its dangers, as we've discussed. Guard your heart against pride, greed, and complacency. Always keep your focus on God, the ultimate provider, and remember that financial freedom is a tool to serve His kingdom.

Stay faithful in your giving, in your work, and in your walk with the Lord. The blessings you've received are not solely for your benefit but are meant to uplift those around you. Share your knowledge, your resources, and your time generously, just as God has been generous with you.

A Life That Reflects God

Your financial freedom is more than a personal achievement; it's a testimony of God's goodness and faithfulness. Let your life reflect His character—His hard work, generosity, humility, fairness, and faithfulness. When people see your life, let them be inspired by the peace, joy, and abundance you've received from walking in God's principles. Let them say, *"Surely, this is someone whom God has blessed."*

The Journey Continues

This is not the end; it's a new beginning. Financial freedom is a foundation upon which you can build a life of greater service, impact, and fulfillment. Continue to grow in wisdom, learn new skills, and seek God's guidance in every decision.

And remember, this journey is not meant to be walked alone. Share what you've learned, encourage others to pursue God's principles, and help them on their own path to financial freedom.

A Prayer for You

As you move forward, I pray that God continues to guide you, bless you, and strengthen you. May He grant you wisdom in your decisions, peace in your heart, and favor in all your endeavors. I pray that you experience His abundant blessings and that you use them to bless others and glorify His name.

May your life be a light to those around you, a living testimony of God's faithfulness and provision. May you flourish in every area, leaving a legacy of faith, integrity, and generosity for generations to come.

Go forth with faith, confidence, and joy, knowing that God is with you every step of the way.

Sincerely,
David Kamali
2025